Editor

Heather Douglas

Managing Editor

Ina Massler Levin, M.A.

Cover Artist

Brenda DiAntonis

Art Production Manager

Kevin Barnes

Imaging

James Edward Grace

Publisher

Mary D. Smith, M.S. Ed.

Grades 1-2

FLUENCY PRACTICE

- Nursery Rhymes
- Poems
- Proverbs
- Readers' Theater
- Songs

BIG RACE TODAY!

Author

Kathleen "Casey" Petersen

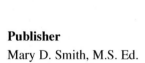

Teacher Created Resources, Inc.

6421 Industry Way

Westminster, CA 92683

www.teachercreated.com

ISBN: 978-1-4206-8040-9

©2006 Teacher Created Resources, Inc.

Reprinted, 2009

Made in U.S.A.

M000169005

Table of Contents

Table of Contents *(cont.)*

Introduction

Fluency is the ability to express oneself easily and gracefully. A fluent reader demonstrates confidence with written material, based on knowledge and practice. *Fluency Practice, Grade 1* offers beginning readers the opportunity to perfect their oral reading skills in a variety of genres, including:

❖ Nursery Rhymes   ❖ Proverbs

❖ Poetry   ❖ Readers' Theater

❖ Songs

As children practice reading each passage aloud, pay attention to their speed. A fluent reader speaks at a comfortable pace, modulating tone periodically. Encourage children to vary their voice when reading dialog, in particular. This is particularly effective in adding interest for both readers and listeners when approaching readers' theater and short stories.

Note whether children hesitate between words. The practice of each piece in this book will ensure smooth, fluid reading at a consistent pace. Pay attention to the number of words pronounced correctly; the fluent child will read with 90–100% accuracy.

Reading aloud can be intimidating for beginners. The pieces in this book are designed to engage children in the reading process with humor, compelling plots, and exciting new words. Encourage children to read each selection several times as a group, in order to build their familiarity with vocabulary and themes. As each child begins to read aloud individually, use positive reinforcement to reward effort and fluency. After each student finishes an oral reading assignment, congratulate the accomplishment and ask the following questions:

✔ *How do you feel about the way you read the piece?*

✔ *Did you read slowly or quickly?*

✔ *Was your reading choppy or smooth?*

✔ *Did you stumble over particular words?*

✔ *How did you feel about your use of expression? Did you vary your tone?*

✔ *Did you show emotion or feeling?*

✔ *How might you read differently next time?*

Use *Fluency Practice, Grade 1* to help create enthusiastic and articulate readers.

Before You Read

It is thought that this rhyme refers to Black Jack, an English pirate who was nimble in escaping capture. Fire or candle leaping was a tradition or sport practiced at fairs.

Jack Be Nimble

Jack be nimble,

Jack be quick,

Jack jump over the candlestick.

Before You Read

Humpty Dumpty was not a person at all, but a cannon that was set up on a wall! The wall was destroyed, so Humpty Dumpty fell and broke. All of the King's horses and men tried to put the cannon back on the wall, but it was too heavy.

Humpty Dumpty

Humpty Dumpty sat on a wall.

Humpty Dumpty had a great fall.

All the king's horses

And all the king's men,

Couldn't put Humpty

Together again.

6

Before You Read

This was a rhyme created to help children learn the days of the week through the use of rhyme. Because Sunday is the Sabbath, there was no reference to a Sunday's child.

Monday's Child

Monday's child is fair of face,

Tuesday's child is full of grace,

Wednesday's child is full of woe,

Thursday's child has far to go,

Friday's child is loving and giving,

Saturday's child works hard for his living,

And the child that is born on the Sabbath day

Is bonny and blithe, and good and gay.

Before You Read

While both flies and bumblebees are insects and pollinators, there are not many more similarities between the two. For instance, while bees feed mainly on nectar and pollen, flies will feast on anything from rotting garbage to manure. Not exactly a match made in heaven!

Fiddle Dee Dee

Fiddle dee dee, fiddle dee dee,

The fly has married the bumblebee.

They went to the church,

And married was she.

The fly has married the bumblebee.

Before You Read

Originally, this poem was Pease Pudding Hot. Pease pudding is a kind of sauce still eaten in the United Kingdom today, made from dried peas and usually served with boiled bacon or a sausage called saveloy. It kept very well in the pot for several days.

Pease Porridge Hot

Pease porridge hot,

Pease porridge cold,

Pease porridge in the pot, nine days old.

Some like it hot,

Some like it cold,

Some like it in the pot, nine days old.

Before You Read

This nursery rhyme is not about any particular person, but a mother's description of a typical boy. It is a rhyme with no known origins, handed down from one generation to the next due to the popularity of the name John. What is unusual is that most old rhymes use the nickname of Jack instead of the name John.

Diddle, Diddle, Dumpling

Diddle, diddle, dumpling,

My son, John,

Went to bed

With his trousers on,

One shoe off

And one shoe on!

Diddle, diddle, dumpling,

My son, John!

Before You Read

This rhyme can be traced back to 1698. It was a tradition to decorate cakes with the name or initial of a child.

Pat-a-Cake

Pat-a-cake, pat-a-cake, baker's man,

Bake me a cake as fast as you can.

Pat it, and prick it, and mark it with a "B,"

And put it in the oven for Baby and me!

Before You Read

It is said that the crooked man is the Scottish General, Sir Alexander Leslie. There had been much arguing and fighting between England and Scotland, and Leslie signed a law to gain religious and political freedom for Scotland. The crooked stile is the border between England and Scotland, and "they all lived together in a crooked little house" means that the two countries had finally agreed on something.

There Was a Crooked Man

There was a crooked man

Who walked a crooked mile.

He found a crooked sixpence

Against a crooked stile.

He bought a crooked cat

Which caught a crooked mouse,

And they all lived together

In a crooked little house.

Before You Read

Jack Horner is said to have been the Bishop of Glastonbury's steward (assistant). King Henry the VIII was looting the monasteries and Glastonbury Abbey was to be next. The Bishop tried to bribe the King with the deeds to 12 estates, which he hid in a pie (for security reasons), and had Horner take them to the King. It is reported that Horner, thinking that the bribes would do no good, took the best one, the "plum," for himself.

Little Jack Horner

Little Jack Horner

Sat in a corner,

Eating a Christmas pie;

He put in his thumb,

And pulled out a plum.

And said, "What a good boy am I!"

Before You Read

The first known publication for this poem is 1728, but it was being played on little toes for generations before that.

This Little Piggy

This little piggy went to market,

This little piggy stayed home,

This little piggy had roast beef,

This little piggy had none,

And this little piggy cried,

"Wee, wee, wee," all the way home.

Before You Read

In the 1700s and 1800s, there were many orphans, and the nickname for orphans was "Tommy Tucker." Orphans often had to beg and sing for food. Orphans rarely married because of their low standing.

Little Tommy Tucker

Little Tommy Tucker sings for his supper,

What shall we give him?

Brown bread and butter.

How shall he cut it-without a knife?

How shall he marry without a wife?

Before You Read

This is a traditional nursery rhyme of unknown origin. References to a china cup and a silver spoon indicate the child is from a wealthy family. A similar saying in reference to wealth is, "He was born with a silver spoon in his mouth."

Sippity Sup

Sippity sup, sippity sup,

Bread and milk from a china cup.

Bread and milk from a bright silver spoon

Made of a piece of the bright silver moon.

Sippity sup, sippity sup,

Sippity, sippity sup.

Before You Read

Queen Elizabeth I's lady-in-waiting had a cat that liked to wander all over Windsor Castle. One time the cat ran under the throne, and when its tail brushed against the Queen's foot, she was startled. The Queen was known as "Good Queen Bess," and instead of doing something mean, she said that the cat could go anywhere in the castle as long as it scared away the mice!

Pussycat, Pussycat

"Pussycat, pussycat, where have you been?"

"I've been up to London to visit the Queen."

"Pussycat, pussycat, what did you there?"

"I frightened a little mouse under her chair."

Before You Read

Of English origin, this is said to be a rhyme for "fathers to trot or bounce children on their knees or feet."

To Market, To Market

To market, to market, to buy a fat pig,

Home again, home again, jiggety jig.

To market, to market, to buy a fat hog,

Home again, home again, jiggety jog.

To market, to market, to buy a plum bun,

Home again, home again, market is done.

Before You Read

The rumor is that this rhyme is about Cardinal Thomas Wolsey during the reign of King Henry VIII. Blue represents the four blue leopards of his coat of arms. "Blow your horn" is about his arrogance and display of wealth. The rhyme asks where he is because he was more concerned with getting things for himself than with helping his country. People could not openly criticize him because they would have been put in prison, had their property taken away, or even been sentenced to death.

Little Boy Blue

Little Boy Blue, come blow your horn,

The sheep's in the meadow, the cow's in the corn;

But where is the boy who looks after the sheep?

He's under the haystack fast asleep.

Will you wake him? No, not I —

For if I do, he's sure to cry.

Before You Read

The story behind this rhyme concerns Miss Patience Muffet's stepfather, Dr. Muffet, a scientist who studied and wrote books about British insects. It is thought that this rhyme was first created in the 1500s.

Little Miss Muffet

Little Miss Muffet, sat on a tuffet,

Eating her curds and whey;

Along came a spider,

Who sat down beside her

And frightened Miss Muffet away.

Before You Read

The rhyme first appeared in print in 1843, but its origins come by word of mouth from long before that date.

The Three Little Kittens

The three little kittens, they lost their mittens,
And they began to cry.
"Oh, Mother dear, we sadly fear,
Our mittens we have lost."
"What! Lost your mittens, you naughty kittens!
Then you shall have no pie."
"Mee-ow, mee-ow, mee-ow. Now we shall have no pie."

The three little kittens, they found their mittens,
And they began to cry,
"Oh, Mother dear, see here, see here,-
For we have found our mittens."
"Put on your mittens, you silly kittens,
And you shall have some pie."
"Purr-r, purr-r, purr-r. Oh, let us have some pie."

The three little kittens, put on their mittens,
And soon ate up the pie,
"Oh, Mother dear, we greatly fear-
That we have soiled our mittens."
"What! Soiled your mittens, you naughty kittens!"
Then they began to sigh,
"Mee-ow, mee-ow, mee-ow." Then they began to sigh.

The three little kittens, they washed their mittens
And hung them out to dry,
"Oh, Mother dear, do you not hear
That we have washed our mittens."
"What! Washed your mittens, you are good kittens.
But I smell a rat close by,"
"Mee-ow, mee-ow, mee-ow. We smell a rat close by."

Before You Read

The first known date of publication of this rhyme is 1765. The phrase, "Hey diddle diddle" can also be found in the works of Shakespeare. Similar phrases such as, "hey nonny no" and "high diddle diddle" can be found in English folk music from the same period. This rhyme appears to be meant as a fun and imaginative piece with no particular meaning.

Hey Diddle, Diddle

Hey diddle, diddle,

The cat and the fiddle,

The cow jumped over the moon.

The little dog laughed

To see such sport,

And the dish ran away

With the spoon.

Before You Read

Before he became a published poet, Carl Sandburg was a day laborer and then worked for a newspaper. "Fog" was a poem he included in his first collection titled CHICAGO POEMS.

Fog

The fog comes

on little cat feet.

It sits looking

over harbor and city

on silent haunches

and then moves on.

~Carl Sandburg

Before You Read

Gelett Burgess wrote this poem in the late 1800s. Later he wrote, "Ah, yes! I wrote 'The Purple Cow' — I'm sorry, now, I wrote it! But I can tell you anyhow, I'll kill you if you quote it!"

The Purple Cow

I never saw a purple cow,

I never hope to see one;

But I can tell you, anyhow

I'd rather see than be one.

~*Gelett Burgess*

Before You Read

This poem is about how weather is unpredictable, but it is also a bit of a tongue twister. The author is unknown.

Weather

Whether the weather be cold,

Or whether the weather be hot

We'll weather the weather,

Whatever the weather,

Whether we like it or not.

Before You Read

Robert Louis Stevenson once said, "It is perhaps a more fortunate destiny to have a taste for collecting shells than to be born a millionaire." He probably did collect shells, and we are glad that he often wrote of the seashore.

At the Seaside

When I was down beside the sea

A wooden spade they gave to me

To dig the sandy shore.

My holes were empty like a cup,

In every hole the sea came up,

Till it could come no more.

~*Robert Louis Stevenson*

Before You Read

Published in the late 1800s–1900, the Goops began as creatures with three eyes and no bones and no mouth. Later people began to think of them as misbehaving children.

The Goops

The Goops they lick their fingers,

And the Goops they lick their knives;

They spill their broth on tablecloths—

Oh they lead disgusting lives!

The Goops they talk while eating,

And loud and fast they chew;

And that is why I'm glad that I

Am not a Goop—are you?

~Gelett Burgess

Before You Read

Longfellow is probably the first American poet to write about American things, such as Paul Revere, Miles Standish, and Hiawatha. In this poem, he writes about the rain coming after "the dust and heat" of summer.

Rain In Summer

How beautiful is the rain!

After the dust and heat,

In the broad and fiery street,

In the narrow lane,

How beautiful is the rain!

How it clatters along the roofs

Like the tramp of hoofs!

How it gushes and struggles out

From the throat of the overflowing spout!

Across the window-pane

It pours and pours;

And swift and wide,

With a muddy tide,

Like a river down the gutter roars

The rain, the welcome rain!

~Henry Wadsworth Longfellow

Before You Read

Shakespeare wrote at least 36 plays, as well as sonnets and poems. He also acted on the London stage. This poem is about faery (fairy) rings, which were unexplained circles in the grass that people would find in the early morning, or circles of mushrooms that would appear overnight.

If You See A Faery Ring

If you see a faery ring

In a field of grass,

Very lightly step around,

Tip-toe as you pass,

Last night faeries frolicked there —

And they're sleeping somewhere near.

If you see a tiny faery,

Lying fast asleep

Shut your eyes

And run away,

Do not stay to peek!

Do not tell

Or you'll break a faery spell.

~William Shakespeare

Before You Read

William Makepeace Thackeray liked to do two things when he was a boy. He liked to draw and he liked to read stories. Here is his poem about the zoo.

At The Zoo

First I saw the white bear, then I saw the black;

Then I saw the camel with a hump upon his back;

Then I saw the grey wolf, with mutton in his maw;

Then I saw the wombat waddle in the straw;

Then I saw the elephant a-waving of his trunk;

Then I saw the monkeys—mercy,

How unpleasantly they—smelt!

~William Makepeace Thackeray

Before You Read

Longfellow's son, Ernest, says that this poem came into his father's mind one night when he was walking back and forth with his crying daughter.

There Was a Little Girl

There was a little girl
Who had a little curl
Right in the middle of her forehead.
When she was good
She was very, very good,
But when she was bad she was horrid.

One day she went upstairs,
When her parents, unawares,
In the kitchen were occupied with meals,
And she stood upon her head
In her little trundle-bed,
And then began hooraying with her heels.

Her mother heard the noise,
And she thought it was the boys
A-playing at a combat in the attic;
But when she climbed the stair,
And found Jemima there,
She took and she did spank her most emphatic.

~Henry Wadsworth Longfellow

Before You Read

It is said that Sarah Catherine Martin took a story that had often been told, but never written on paper, and made it into a story. Her story was published in 1805 by John Harris. The first publication was a picture book with illustrations of Old Mother Hubbard and her dog. The publisher liked to have the illustrations colored by a group of young people who sat around the table filling in the colors with watercolors. The book was a bestseller!

The Comic Adventures of Old Mother Hubbard and Her Dog

Old Mother Hubbard
Went to the cupboard,
To give the poor dog a bone;
When she came there
The cupboard was bare,
And so the poor dog had none.

She went to the baker's
To buy him some bread;
When she got back
The dog was dead.

She went to the undertaker's
To buy him a coffin;
When she got back
The dog was laughing.

She took a clean dish
To get him some tripe;
When she came back
He was smoking a pipe.

The Comic Adventures of
Old Mother Hubbard and Her Dog (cont.)

She went to the tailor's
To buy him a coat;
When she came back
He was riding a goat.

She went to the hatter's
To buy him a hat;
When she came back
He was feeding the cat.

She went to the barber's
To buy him a wig;
When she came back
He was dancing a jig.

She went to the cobbler's
To buy him some shoes;
When she came back
He was reading the news.

She went to the hosier's
To buy him some hose;
When she came back
He was dressed in his clothes.

The dame made a curtsy,
The dog made made a bow;
The dame said, "Your servant,"
The dog said, "Bow-wow."

~Sarah Catherine Martin

Before You Read

Sarah Josepha Hale wrote at least 50 books (novels and poetry) and edited publications. Her poem, "Mary's Lamb," is probably the most well-known of all of her work. She is also known for asking President Abraham Lincoln for a national Thanksgiving Day, so she is responsible for our taking the third Thursday of each November to spend with our families and give thanks.

Mary's Lamb

Mary had a little lamb,
Its fleece was white as snow,
And everywhere that Mary went
The lamb was sure to go;

> He followed her to school one day—
> That was against the rule,
> It made the children laugh and play
> To see a lamb at school.

And so the teacher turned him out,
But still he lingered near,
And waited patiently about,
Till Mary did appear.

> And then he ran to her and laid
> His head upon her arm,
> As if he said, "I'm not afraid—
> You'll shield me from all harm."

"What makes the lamb love Mary so?"
The little children cry;
"Oh, Mary loves the lamb, you know,"
The teacher did reply,

> "And, you, each gentle animal
> In confidence may bind,
> And make it follow at your call,
> If you are always kind."

~Sarah Josepha Hale

Before You Read

A poem of unknown origin, written circa 1745. When children have jumped and tumbled all day, and night has come, it must be time for them to tumble to bed.

Tumbling

In jumping and tumbling

We spend the whole day,

Till night by arriving

Has finished our play.

What then? One and all,

There's no more to be said,

As we tumbled all day,

So we tumble to bed.

~Anonymous

Before You Read

Stevenson had health problems as a child, became an attorney in 1875, but he never practiced law, choosing, instead, to write. He wrote Kidnapped, *and* Treasure Island. *"The Swing" appeared in* A Child's Garden of Verses *in 1885. It's good to know that riding on a swing is still a pleasant thing to do!*

The Swing

How do you like to go up in a swing,

Up in the air so blue?

Oh, I do think it the pleasantest thing

Ever a child can do!

Up in the air and over the wall,

Till I can see so wide,

Rivers and trees and cattle and all

Over the countryside—

Till I look down on the garden green,

Down on the roof so brown—

Up in the air I go flying again,

Up in the air and down!

~Robert Louis Stevenson

Before You Read

This is a poem of unknown origins. It can be sung to the tune of "Mulberry Bush," and has accompanying movements (in brackets) for each line of the poem.

The Elephant

The elephant goes like this and

That, [slap right leg and slap left leg]

He's terribly big and terribly

Fat. [Hands up tall and out wide]

He has no fingers, he has no

Toes, [point to toes]

But goodness, gracious, what a

NOSE! [Swoop down arms and make a trunk.]

~Anonymous

Before You Read

No one knows who first created this poem, but it is thought to have been created in America in the late 1800s. It has been told to children for generations, and many children have made wishes on stars as a result.

Star Light, Star Bright

Star light, star bright,

First star I see tonight,

I wish I may, I wish I might,

Have the wish I wish tonight.

~Anonymous

Before You Read

Before people had regular newspapers, radio, television, and the Internet, they relied on the town crier to wander through the town calling out the news and the time. William Miller wrote this version of a child's town crier in 1841.

Wee Willie Winkie

Wee Willie Winkie

Runs through the town,

Upstairs and downstairs

In his nightgown.

Rapping at the windows,

Crying through the lock,

"Are the children all in bed?"

For it's now eight o'clock.

~William Miller

Before You Read

*This is thought to be a children's song from the 1880s by George Cooper.
It is full of personification as the wind speaks to the leaves and tells them
to put on their autumn dresses.*

An Autumn Greeting

"Come," said the Wind to the Leaves one day.

"Come over the meadow and we will play.

Put on your dresses of red and gold.

For summer is gone and the days grow cold."

~George Cooper

40

Before You Read

In this poem, Stevenson very effectively speaks as a young boy looking forward to being a grown up man telling others not to mess with his toys.

Looking Forward

When I am grown to man's estate

I shall be very proud and great,

And tell the other girls and boys

Not to meddle with my toys.

~*Robert Louis Stevenson*

Before You Read

This is a poem of unknown origin. It is likely that it was posted on the wall of a classroom to remind students to be like the clock with hands, ready to do the right things each day.

The Clock

There's a neat little clock,

In the schoolroom it stands,

And points to the time,

With its two little hands.

And may we like the clock,

Keep a face clean and bright,

With hands ever ready,

To do what is right.

~Anonymous

Before You Read

Perhaps it is because Robert Louis Stevenson began to write at such an early age that he writes so well of the memories of childhood. Perhaps it is because he often had health problems that he developed such an imagination and such sensitive senses to notice the everyday things.

Auntie's Skirts

Whenever Auntie moves around,

Her dresses make a curious sound,

They trail behind her up the floor,

And trundle after through the door.

~*Robert Louis Stevenson*

Before You Read

The author of "Pretty Cow" also wrote "Twinkle, Twinkle Little Star." In this poem she is grateful for the family cow that gives her milk each day. She knew the cow and her milk so well that she even knew what the cow should or should not eat to make the milk taste sweet.

Pretty Cow

Thank you, pretty cow, that made

Pleasant milk to soak my bread

Every day and every night,

Warm, and fresh, and sweet, and white.

Do not chew the hemlock rank,

Growing on the weedy bank;

But the yellow cowslips eat,

That will make it very sweet.

Where the purple violet grows,

Where the bubbling water flows,

Where the grass is fresh and fine,

Pretty cow, go there and dine.

~Jane Taylor

Before You Read

A wren is a small, brown songbird with a short tail. Only four gathered in this tree before they all flew away. This poem can be done as a finger play by holding up the correct number of fingers.

Four Wrens

There were two wrens upon a tree,

Whistle and I'll come to thee;

Another came, and there were three,

Whistle and I'll come to thee;

Another came and there were four,

You needn't whistle any more,

For being frightened, off they flew,

And there are none to show to you.

~Anonymous

Before You Read

These two proverbs are both about feathered friends. The first one states that having one bird already is better than having two in a bush, because one is a sure thing and the other two might fly away. The second proverb is similar because it is telling us that we can't count the eggs to determine how many chickens we have since not all the eggs will hatch into chickens.

Bird Proverbs

A bird in the hand is worth two in a bush.

Don't count your chickens before they hatch.

Before You Read

These are two proverbs about danger! The first one is about doing something to make sure you are safe, like buckling your seatbelt. The second one is about how sometimes cats, being very curious about things, crawl into places where they should not go and then they might become injured or worse. It is a proverb that warns us to be careful and not be like a cat.

Proverbs About Danger

Better safe than sorry.

Curiosity killed the cat.

Before You Read

These two proverbs are about golden things and money. Sometimes people think that the only way to make their piggy banks heavier is to work more and make more money. Sometimes saving, instead of spending, is the best way to have more money. And just because something looks shiny and glitters does not mean that it is real gold. This can be about people, too!

Money Proverbs

A penny saved is
a penny gained.

Scottish Proverb

All that glitters
is not gold.

Before You Read

These food proverbs are about different things. An apple a day can make a person very healthy so that he or she doesn't need a doctor. And once the milk is spilled, it makes no sense to cry about it. It is already spilled. People say the second proverb sometimes when something happens, or something is said, and it is too late to undo what has been done or said.

Food Proverbs

An apple a day keeps the doctor away.

It is no use crying over spilt milk.

Before You Read

These two proverbs are about work and how to get it done better. The first one is about how work is done more quickly when there are helping hands. The second one is about how, if we take care of something early on, we won't have to spend as much time taking care of it later.

Proverbs About Work

Many hands make light work.

A stitch in time saves nine.

Before You Read

These colorful proverbs are about how we see things. Even though clouds might look gray and dark, they look different from a different angle. Some things that trouble us might also bring us good things. And sometimes we think that other people have it better than we do, and that is why people say that the grass is greener over there, on the other side of the fence.

Colorful Proverbs

Every cloud has a silver lining.

English Proverb

The grass is always greener on the other side of the fence.

Before You Read

Friends are important. If a best friend lives far away, it is not enough to keep us from going to see him. And the best way to know how to treat other people is to think of how we like to be treated.

Friend Proverbs

The road to a friend's house is never long.

Danish proverb

Do unto others as you would have them to do unto you.

Before You Read

The first bird proverb is about how those who do things early usually get what they want. The second bird proverb is about how we tend to make friends with those who are most like us.

More Bird Proverbs

The early bird catches the worm.

Birds of a feather flock together.

Before You Read

The original tale of The Three Billy Goats Gruff is a Norwegian fairy tale by Peter Christen Asbjornsen.

The Three Billy Goats Gruff

Teacher: The three goats are hungry. They want something to eat.

Students: Trip, trap, trip, trap.

Teacher: Look under the bridge! Look out for the troll!

Students: Trip, trap, trip, trap.

Teacher: Over the bridge, the little goat goes.

Students: Trip, trap, trip, trap.

Teacher: Over the bridge, the next goat goes.

Students: Trip, trap, trip, trap.

Teacher: Over the bridge, the biggest goat goes.

Students: Trip, trap, trip, trap.

Teacher: Away from the bridge runs the troll, and the goats have their lunch.

Students: Trip, trap, trip, trap.

Teacher: The story of the three goats comes to an end.

All: Snip, snap, snout! This tale's told out!

Before You Read

The original tale was of a fleeing pancake! The tale has been told all over the world with many Irish, Scandinavian, Dutch, German, and Russian versions. Originally, the pancake was fleeing from a grandmother, a mother, and her little girl.

The Gingerbread Man

Students: Run, run, as fast as you can. You can't catch me, I'm the Gingerbread Man!

Teacher: Here comes the old woman and the old man.

Students: Run, run, as fast as you can.

Teacher: Here comes a pig, Mr. Gingerbread Man.

Students: Run, run, as fast as you can.

Teacher: Here comes a dog, Mr. Gingerbread Man.

Students: Run, run, as fast as you can.

Teacher: Here comes a horse, Mr. Gingerbread Man.

Students: Run, run, as fast as you can.

Teacher: Here comes a cow, Mr. Gingerbread Man.

Students: Run, run, as fast as you can.

Teacher: But the fox caught you, Mr. Gingerbread Man!

Before You Read

The Mayan version of this story is "The Rabbit and the Crab." This is a tale that has been told in many ways. The most well known version is the fable of Aesop who lived as a slave around the 6th century B.C.

The Hare and the Tortoise

Teacher: Hare and Tortoise had a race.

Students: Go! Go! Slow and steady wins the race!

Teacher: Hare was fast. Tortoise was slow.

Students: Go! Go! Slow and steady wins the race!

Teacher: Hare was winning. Tortoise was walking.

Students: Go! Go! Slow and steady wins the race!

Teacher: Hare was winning. Tortoise kept walking.

Students: Go! Go! Slow and steady wins the race!

Teacher: Hare was sleeping. Tortoise kept walking.

Students: Go! Go! Slow and steady wins the race!

Teacher: Hare woke up. Tortoise kept walking.

Students: Go! Go! Slow and steady wins the race!

Teacher: Tortoise kept walking and won the race!

Students: Hooray! Hooray! Slow and steady won the race!

Before You Read

This is a tale that was possibly first published in 1849 by James Orchard Halliwell. Others have told this tale since. Joseph Jacobs made it popular in his book published in 1898, English Fairy Tales. *Even Walt Disney has a version in his 1933 cartoon "Silly Symphonies."*

The Three Little Pigs

Teacher: One pig built his house of straw.

Students: Oh, no! Oh, no!

Teacher: One pig built his house of sticks.

Students: Oh, no! Oh, no!

Teacher: One pig built his house of bricks.

Students: Smart pig! Smart pig!

Teacher: Then the wolf came to blow them down!

Students: Huff, puff! Huff, puff!

Teacher: Down went the houses of straw and sticks.

Students: Huff, puff! Huff, puff!

Teacher: But he couldn't blow down that house of bricks.

Students: Huff, puff! Huff, puff!

Teacher: Who's afraid of the big, bad wolf?

Students: Not us! Not us!

Before You Read

The little red hen's tale has similar origins to those of the three little pigs' tale. In both cases, Joseph Jacobs was the first to publish the tale. And in both cases, there have been many versions that followed.

The Little Red Hen

All: Little Red Hen has found some wheat.

Teacher: Who will help me plant the wheat, so we may have bread to eat?

Students: "Quack, not I," said the duck. "Meow, not I," said the cat. "Woof, not I," said the dog.

Teacher: Then I shall do it myself.

Who will help me water the wheat, so we may have bread to eat?

Students: "Quack, not I," said the duck. "Meow, not I," said the cat. "Woof, not I," said the dog.

Teacher: Then I shall do it myself.

Who will help me sow the wheat, so we may have bread to eat?

Students: "Quack, not I," said the duck. "Meow, not I," said the cat. "Woof, not I," said the dog.

The Little Red Hen (cont.)

Teacher: Then I shall do it myself.

Who will help me cut the wheat, so we may have bread to eat?

Students: "Quack, not I," said the duck. "Meow, not I," said the cat. "Woof, not I," said the dog.

Teacher: Then I shall do it myself.

Who will help me grind the wheat, so we may have bread to eat?

Students: "Quack, not I," said the duck. "Meow, not I," said the cat. "Woof, not I," said the dog.

Teacher: Then I shall do it myself.

Who will help me bake the bread?

Students: "Quack, not I," said the duck. "Meow, not I," said the cat. "Woof, not I," said the dog.

Teacher: Then I shall do it myself.

When the bread was done

Her friends did want to eat,

But the Little Red Hen

Ate the whole treat!

Before You Read

This tale has been around for centuries. In the earliest recorded versions the intruder was either a fox or an old woman. Eventually the intruder became a little girl named "Silver Hair" in a version published in 1849. Later, she became "Goldilocks."

Goldilocks and the Three Bears

All: The three bears went for a walk, and in came Goldilocks.

Teacher: Goldilocks tasted Papa Bear's porridge.

Students: This porridge is too hot!

Teacher: Goldilocks tasted Mama Bear's porridge.

Students: This porridge is too cold.

Teacher: Goldilocks tasted Baby Bear's porridge.

Students: This porridge is just right!

Teacher: And she ate it all up! Then, Goldilocks sat in Papa Bear's chair.

Students: This chair is too hard.

Teacher: Goldilocks sat in Mama Bear's chair.

Students: This chair is too soft.

Teacher: Goldilocks sat in Baby Bear's chair.

Students: This chair is just right!

Goldilocks and the Three Bears *(cont.)*

Teacher: But she broke the chair, so she went upstairs to the bedroom. Goldilocks crawled into Papa Bear's bed.

Students: This bed is too hard.

Teacher: Goldilocks crawled into Mama Bear's bed.

Students: This bed is too soft.

Teacher: Goldilocks crawled into Baby Bear's bed.

Students: This bed is just right!

Teacher: Goldilocks sighed and went right to sleep.

The Bears came home from their walk.

Teacher: Papa Bear said, "Somebody has been eating my porridge."

Students: Who could it be?

Teacher: Mama Bear said, "Somebody has been eating MY porridge."

Students: Who could it be?

Teacher: Baby Bear said, "Somebody has been eating my porridge, and waaahhh, it's all gone!"

Students: Oh, no! Oh, no!

Teacher: The Bears went into the living room. Papa Bear said, "Somebody has been sitting in my chair."

Goldilocks and the Three Bears *(cont.)*

Students: Who could it be?

Teacher: Mama Bear said, "Somebody has been sitting in MY chair."

Students: Who could it be?

Teacher: Baby Bear said, "Somebody has been sitting in MY chair, and waaaahhh, it's broken into pieces!"

Students: Oh, no! Oh, no!

Teacher: The Bears went upstairs to the bedroom. Papa Bear said, "Somebody has been sleeping in my bed."

Students: Who could it be?

Teacher: Mama Bear said, "Somebody has been sleeping in MY bed."

Students: Who could it be?

Teacher: Baby Bear said, "Somebody has been sleeping in my bed, and HEY, there she is!"

Students: Oh, no! Oh, no!

Teacher: At that, Goldilocks woke up, saw the three bears, jumped up and ran all the way home as fast as she could run!

Before You Read

This tale became popular when published in Hans Christian Andersen's New Tales *in 1844, but it had been published earlier than that.*

The Ugly Duckling

Teacher: A mother duck sat in a meadow, waiting for her eggs to hatch. At last she heard a crack!

Students: Peep, peep, peep!

Teacher: Eight eggs cracked!

Students: Peep, peep, peep! What a big world!

Teacher: The mother duck let her ducklings rest while she told them about the big world. Then she said, "Let's take a walk, are we all ready?"

Students: Peep, peep, peep!

Teacher: The mother duck saw that there was still one egg that hadn't hatched yet, so she sighed and sat down to wait some more.

Students: Peep, peep, peep!

Teacher: Finally the egg hatched and out came two big feet and a head that wasn't soft and fuzzy like the other ducklings.

"What an ugly duckling!"

Students: Peep, peep, peep, what an ugly duckling!

Teacher: The mother duck waddled to the pond and her ducklings followed her.

Students: Peep, peep, peep, can the ugly duckling swim?

The Ugly Duckling *(cont.)*

Teacher: He sure is ugly, but look at him swim!

Students: Peep, peep, peep, look at him swim!

Teacher: The next day the mother duck took her ducklings to see the farm animals. A goose looked at the ducklings and said, "Why is this one so ugly?" And then she bit him on the neck!

Students: Oh, my! Peep, peep, peep, she bit him on the neck!

Teacher: The mother duck said, "You leave him alone you mean old bird. He may not be pretty, but he is very kind and a wonderful swimmer!"

Students: Peep, peep, peep! He's kind and a wonderful swimmer!

Teacher: But that didn't stop the barnyard animals from being mean to him. The Ugly Duckling was so sad that he decided to fly away.

Students: Peep, peep, peep! He flew away!

Teacher: He flew through storms and rested near ponds and was so sad and lonely.

Students: Peep, peep, peep. So sad and lonely.

64

The Ugly Duckling *(cont.)*

Teacher: The summer came and went, and then it was fall, and the leaves were falling and the ugly duckling was still sad and lonely.

Students: Peep, peep, peep. So sad and lonely.

Teacher: But one day, he saw a flock of beautiful swans come out of the bushes and fly away!

Students: Peep, peep, peep! Swans!

Teacher: The Ugly Duckling sadly sat by the cold pond and looked down. It was then that he saw himself reflected in the water!

Students: Peep, peep, peep! I'm a swan!

Teacher: The Ugly Duckling wasn't a duck, he was a swan, and he was beautiful. He spread his wings and joined his swan family to fly to a warmer climate.

Students: He was a beautiful swan!

Before You Read

The most popular early version of this tale is the one that Hans Christian Andersen wrote, "The Princess on the Pea," in the book, Tales Told For Children, *published in 1835. But there were many versions that were told before then. In the earliest versions, the princess is told by a friend that there will be a pea placed under all of her mattresses, and so she is able to pretend to have not slept a wink.*

The Princess and the Pea

Teacher: There once was a prince who wanted to marry a real princess.

Students: A really, truly, real princess!

Teacher: The prince traveled all over the world and met many princesses. But it was difficult to tell if they were real or not.

Students: A really, truly, real princess!

Teacher: He just wasn't sure, so he came home and felt sad because he really wanted to find a real princess.

Students: A really, truly, real princess!

Teacher: One night there was a terrible storm!

Students: Oh, no! A terrible storm!

Teacher: There was thunder and lightning!

Students: Crash, bang!

Teacher: There was a knock on the door.

Students: Rappity-Rap, Rap!

Teacher: The king answered the door and there stood a wet girl! She said she was a princess!

Students: A really, truly, real princess?

The Princess and the Pea (cont.)

Teacher: The Queen didn't believe her, and she had a plan. She put a pea on the bottom of the bed, and then put 20 mattresses and 20 feather beds on top.

Students: Oh my! Why?

Teacher: The Queen thought that if the girl was a real princess, she would not be able to sleep with a pea under the 20 mattresses and the 20 feather beds.

Students: Twenty mattresses, 20 feather beds, and one pea!

Teacher: In the morning the Queen asked the princess how she slept.

The princess said, "I have scarcely closed my eyes all night. Heaven only knows what was in the bed, but I was lying on something so hard, that I am sore all over, and terribly exhausted!"

Students: Oh, no! Oh, no!

Teacher: When the prince heard this, he knew she was a real princess.

Students: A really, truly, real princess!

Teacher: He asked her to marry him and they lived happily ever after!

Students: And what about the pea?

Teacher: It was placed under glass in a museum!

Before You Read

The origin of this tale is unknown, but it is thought that it came to England from invading Norsemen. The earliest published version is thought to be "The History of Jack and the Giants," printed by J. White in 1711.

Jack and the Beanstalk

Teacher: Once upon a time a poor widow lived with her son, Jack, and their cow, Milky. They sold milk from the cow each day, and that is how they lived. But one morning, Milky had no milk!

Students: No milk? What will we do?

Teacher: The mother decided to sell the cow so they could buy some food. Jack took the cow to the market.

Students: To market, to market, to sell the milk cow!

Teacher: On the way to the market, Jack met a man who traded the cow for magic beans!

Students: Magic beans that grow right up to the sky!

Teacher: When Jack got home, his mother asked him what he got for the cow. When he showed her the beans, she was angry and threw them out of the window!

Students: Magic beans that grow right up to the sky!

Teacher: Jack had trouble sleeping because he was hungry and he thought about his mistake most of the night. But when he woke up, there outside was the biggest beanstalk he had ever seen!

Students: Magic beans that grow right up to the sky!

Teacher: Jack climbed out his window and onto the beanstalk and climbed all the way to the sky where he found a giant woman on the doorstep of a very tall house. Jack was so hungry, he asked her for something to eat.

Jack and the Beanstalk *(cont.)*

Students: I'm so very hungry. Can I have some breakfast?

Teacher: The woman told Jack that her husband was an ogre and Jack would be breakfast if he didn't run away!

Students: I'm so very hungry. I can't run away!

Teacher: The woman took pity on Jack and fed him some bread and cheese, and then they heard the ogre coming!

Students: THUMP, THUMP, THUMP!

Teacher: She hid Jack in the oven, and the ogre came into the kitchen!

Students: Fee-fi-fo-fum!

Teacher: The ogre fell asleep while counting his bags of gold.

Students: (Snoring sounds)

Teacher: As Jack escaped, he took a bag of gold with him. When his mother saw the bag of gold Jack said, "I told you it was a magic beanstalk!"

Students: A magic beanstalk that reaches the sky!

Teacher: After they ran out of gold, Jack climbed the beanstalk again. Again he hid in the oven when the ogre arrived.

Students: Fee-fi-fo-fum!

Teacher: This time Jack saw the ogre say to a hen, "Lay," and there appeared a golden egg!

Students: A hen that lays golden eggs!

Teacher: When the ogre fell asleep...

Jack and the Beanstalk *(cont.)*

Students: (Snoring sounds)

Teacher: Jack took the hen!

Students: A hen that lays golden eggs!

Teacher: Jack went down the beanstalk and showed his mother the hen. He said, "Lay," and a golden egg magically appeared!

Students: A hen that lays golden eggs!

Teacher: After a while, Jack wanted more, so up the beanstalk he went and he hid in the ogre's house.

Students: A magic beanstalk that reaches the sky!

Teacher: This time he saw a golden harp that sang beautifully. When the ogre fell asleep...

Students: (Snoring sounds)

Teacher: ...Jack took the golden harp. This time the ogre woke up!

Students: Oh, no! Oh, no!

Teacher: The ogre started to chase Jack down the beanstalk! He called to his mother to cut it with an ax!

Students: Oh, no! Oh, no!

Teacher: Jack fell to the ground!

Students: Ow!

Teacher: When Jack woke up, he promised his mother that he would never be so greedy again.

Students: Hooray for Jack!

Before You Read

This is a tale that is brand new. The author fell asleep one night after spending a day working with poetry and rhymes and the story unfolded before her.

Saggy Aggie

Teacher: Aggie was a dog. Aggie was a saggy dog. Everyone called Aggie Saggy Aggie.

Students: Saggy Aggie was a saggy dog!

Teacher: Saggy Aggie's owner was named Maggie. Maggie wore baggy clothes, so everyone called Maggie, Baggy Maggie.

Students: Baggy Maggie wore baggy clothes!

Teacher: When Baggy Maggie walked Saggy Aggie, everyone said, "There goes Baggy Maggie and Saggy Aggie!"

Students: There goes Baggy Maggie and Saggy Aggie!

Teacher: One day when Saggy Aggie and Baggy Maggie were out walking, they ran into Shabby Tabby.

Students: Saggy Aggie, Baggy Maggie, and Shabby Tabby!

Teacher: Tabby was an orange striped cat who had lost some of her fur one day when she got caught in a garbage truck, so that is why everyone started to call her Shabby Tabby.

Students: Saggy Aggie, Baggy Maggie, and Shabby Tabby!

Teacher: Shabby Tabby asked Saggy Aggie and Baggy Maggie, "Can I join you for your walk?"

Students: Saggy Aggie, Baggy Maggie, and Shabby Tabby!

Teacher: Saggy Aggie said, "Ro-woof!" and Baggy Maggie said, "Of course!" And Saggy Aggie, Baggy Maggie, and Shabby Tabby went walking to the park.

Students: Saggy Aggie, Baggy Maggie, and Shabby Tabby!

Teacher: At the park they met Raggie. Raggie was a ragtag cat who was sold in a tag sale, so, everyone called Raggie, Raggie Taggie.

Students: Saggy Aggie, Baggy Maggie, Shabby Tabby, and Raggie Taggie!

Saggy Aggie *(cont.)*

Teacher: Raggie Taggie was wearing a scrap of calico around his neck and he asked if Saggy Aggie, Baggy Maggie, and Shabby Tabby would care to join him downtown for a dip in the fountain. It was a warm day so Saggy Aggie, Baggy Maggie, and Shabby Tabby said they would.

Students: Saggy Aggie, Baggy Maggie, Shabby Tabby, and Raggie Taggie!

Teacher: At the fountain they met Happy. Happy was a happy old man who loved to sit at the fountain and feed the pigeons. Most of his front teeth were missing, so everyone called him Gappy Happy. When he saw Saggy Aggie, Baggy Maggie, Shabby Tabby, and Raggie Taggie coming his way, he clapped his hands with joy and did his best to say, "Greetings Saggy Aggie, Baggy Maggie, Shabby Tabby, and Raggie Taggie!"

Students: Saggy Aggie, Baggy Maggie, Shabby Tabbie, Raggie Taggie, and Gappy Happy!

Teacher: Saggy Aggie, Baggy Maggie, Shabby Tabby, Raggie Taggie, and Gappy Happy had a wonderful time feeding the pigeons (Shabbie Tabby and Raggie Taggie did not try to eat the pigeons because they preferred seafood).

Students: Saggy Aggie, Baggy Maggie, Shabby Tabby, Raggie Taggie, and Gappy Happy!

Teacher: Soon the mayor of the city came to the fountain. He was practicing his speech for that night in the town square. He said, "Well, hello! If it isn't Saggy Aggie, Baggy Maggie, Shabby Tabbie, Raggie Taggie, and Gappy Happy!"

Students: Saggy Aggie, Baggy Maggie, Shabby Tabby, Raggie Taggie, and Gappy Happy!

Teacher: And those were the last words that the Mayor said for a month! His tongue got so tangled that it took all of the city's best doctors and nurses to untangle it. He was unable to give his speech, so all of the townspeople cheered and played in the park all night long!

Before You Read

This is a nursery rhyme and song of unknown origins. Sometimes this song is called the "Itsy Bitsy Spider" or the "Eensy, Weensy Spider." Why did the spider climb up the waterspout? Spiders climb up things in order to spread out and away (using their webs) from their brothers and sisters so that they won't have to fight over food.

Eency Weency Spider

The eency weency spider

Climbed up the water spout;

Down came the rain

And washed poor Eency out;

Out came the sun

And dried up all the rain;

And the eency weency spider

Climbed up the spout again.

Before You Read

The earliest publication date for this rhyme or song is 1744. It was created during the middle ages when wool was very important to the economy of Europe.

Baa, Baa, Black Sheep

Baa, baa, black sheep

Have you any wool?

Yes, sir, yes, sir,

Three bags full;

One for my master,

One for my dame,

And one for the little boy

Who lives down the lane.

Before You Read

Originally a nursery rhyme from France, the first publication date is 1795. It was originally "Jack and Gill." It is said that Jack represents King Louis XVI, who lost his crown. Queen Marie Antoinette, who came tumbling after, is Jill.

Jack and Jill

Jack and Jill went up the hill,

To fetch a pail of water.

Jack fell down

And broke his crown,

And Jill came tumbling after.

Before You Read

This song was originally a poem, written by Jane Taylor in 1806. The tune to which it is sung today was very similar to a song that French children liked to sing, "Ah! Vous Dirai-je, Maman." When he was seventeen years old, Mozart used the tune in one of his piano compositions.

Twinkle, Twinkle

Twinkle, twinkle, little star,
How I wonder what you are,
Up above the clouds so high,
Like a diamond in the sky.

When the blazing sun is gone,
When he nothing shines upon,
Then you show your little light,
Twinkle, twinkle, all the night.

Then the traveller in the dark,
Thanks you for your tiny spark,
He could not see which way to go,
If you did not twinkle so.

In the dark blue sky you keep,
And often through my curtains peep,
For you never shut your eye,
Till the sun is in the sky.

As your bright and tiny spark,
Lights the traveller in the dark —
Though I know not what you are,
Twinkle, twinkle, little star.

~Jane Taylor

Before You Read

Muffins baked on hot griddles were very popular in 19th century England. These were the predecessors of today's "English muffins." Muffin men were quite common in English society, peddling their fresh muffins door to door.

The Muffin Man

Oh, do you know the muffin man,

The muffin man, the muffin man,

Oh, do you know the muffin man,

That lives on Drury Lane?

Oh, yes, I know the muffin man,

The muffin man, the muffin man.

Oh, yes, I know the muffin man,

That lives on Drury Lane!

This Old Man

This old man, he played one,
He played knick-knack on his thumb,
With a knick-knack, paddy-whack,
Give the dog a bone;
This old man came rolling home.

This old man, he played two,
He played knick-knack on his shoe,
With a knick-knack, paddy-whack,
Give the dog a bone;
This old man came rolling home.

This old man, he played three,
He played knick-knack on his knee,
With a knick-knack, paddy-whack,
Give the dog a bone;
This old man came rolling home.

This old man, he played four,
He played knick-knack on his door,
With a knick-knack, paddy-whack,
Give the dog a bone;
This old man came rolling home.

This old man, he played five,
He played knick-knack on his hive,
With a knick-knack, paddy-whack,
Give the dog a bone;
This old man came rolling home.

This Old Man (cont.)

This old man, he played six,
He played knick-knack on his sticks,
With a knick-knack, paddy-whack,
Give the dog a bone;
This old man came rolling home.

> This old man, he played seven,
> He played knick-knack with his pen,
> With a knick-knack, paddy-whack,
> Give the dog a bone;
> This old man came rolling home.

This old man, he played eight,
He played knick-knack on his gate,
With a knick-knack, paddy-whack,
Give the dog a bone;
This old man came rolling home.

> This old man, he played nine,
> He played knick-knack, rise and shine,
> With a knick-knack, paddy-whack,
> Give the dog a bone;
> This old man came rolling home.

This old man, he played ten,
He played knick-knack on his hen,
With a knick-knack, paddy-whack,
Give the dog a bone;
This old man came rolling home.
This old man came rolling home.

Before You Read

From 1665 and the Great Plague of London, this song represents the symptoms of the disease: the rosy red rash in the shape of a ring, the pockets full of sweet smelling herbs (it was thought that bad smells caused the spread of the disease), the ashes (cremation) and all fall down (the large number of deaths due to the Bubonic Plague).

Ring Around the Rosie

Ring around the rosie,

A pocket full of posies,

Ashes, ashes,

We all fall down!

Before You Read

There are actually two versions of this verse, the other being titled, "London Bridge is Broken Down." That version is about Queen Anne Boleyn. This version began early in London's history when the bridge was made of wood and clay. It fell many times due to Viking invasion, fires, etc. It was also rebuilt many times.

London Bridge

London Bridge is falling down,

Falling down, falling down,

London Bridge is falling down,

My fair lady.

Take a key and lock her up,

Lock her up, lock her up,

Take a key and lock her up,

My fair lady.

Before You Read

This is a lullaby to sing to a baby. The earliest recorded publication of the lyrics is 1784.

Cry Baby Bunting

Cry Baby Bunting

Daddy's gone a-hunting,

Gone to fetch a rabbit skin,

To wrap the Baby Bunting in,

Cry Baby Bunting.

Before You Read

This song was first published in 1744. It is thought to be a silly song for learning how to tell time. It is probably an American song due to the use of "hickory" which is a kind of tree in Virginia, and "dock" which is a weed used by Native Americans for healing purposes.

Hickory Dickory Dock

Hickory dickory dock,

The mouse ran up the clock,

The clock struck one,

The mouse ran down,

Hickory dickory dock!

Before You Read

This is a song of unknown origins. It's fun to sing it as a round. Recently, a man named Emmanuel Coindre actually rowed across the Pacific Ocean! He set off from a port in Japan, and 129 days later, crossed into U.S. waters.

Row, Row, Row Your Boat

Row, row, row your boat,

Gently down the stream,

Merrily, merrily, merrily, merrily,

Life is but a dream.

Before You Read

This rhyme was written, so it is told, by a dad who watched his children play. It was written in 1797 England. The girls wanted the boys to go play soldiers somewhere else, so, they would pretend that they were about to have a pretend tea party, "Polly put the kettle on." The boys would disappear, not wanting to have anything to do with a tea party! Once the boys were gone, Susan (Sukey) would remove the kettle from the stove and the girls would play peacefully. Since then, the song has been popular in many versions, including bluegrass!

Polly Put the Kettle On

Polly put the kettle on,

Polly put the kettle on,

Polly put the kettle on,

We'll all have tea.

Sukey take it off again,

Sukey take it off again,

Sukey take it off again,

They've all gone away.

Before You Read

This is an anonymous silly song that can be sung to the tune of "Polly Wolly Doodle." There is a novel called, How To Eat Fried Worms, *by Thomas Rockwell, which includes even more disgusting rhymes.*

Worms

Nobody likes me

Everyone hates me

Think I'll go eat some worms!

Big fat juicy ones

Little tiny skinny ones,

Think I'll go eat some worms!

Before You Read

This rhyme comes from the time of King Henry the VII. The "farmer's wife" is the King's daughter, and the "three blind mice" would be three noblemen who were convicted of plotting against the Queen.

Three Blind Mice

Three blind mice,

Three blind mice,

See how they run!

See how they run!

They all ran after the farmer's wife,

She cut off their tails with a carving knife,

Did you ever see such a sight in your life,

As three blind mice?

Before You Read

This is a song of unknown origin, but it has been adapted by many, many writers who have made it into books, toys, board games, books, and even karaoke!

The Wheels on the Bus

The wheels on the bus go round and round,
Round and round, round and round.
The wheels on the bus go round and round,
All through the town.

The wipers on the bus go swish, swish, swish;
Swish, swish, swish; swish, swish, swish.
The wipers on the bus go swish, swish, swish,
All through the town.

The horn on the bus goes beep, beep, beep;
Beep, beep, beep; beep, beep, beep.
The horn on the bus goes beep, beep, beep,
All through the town.

The driver on the bus says, "Move on back,
move on back, move on back."
The driver on the bus says, "Move on back,"
All through the town.

The babies on the bus say, "Wah, wah, wah;
Wah, wah, wah; wah, wah, wah."
The babies on the bus say, "Wah, wah, wah,"
All through the town.

The mommies on the bus say, "Shush, shush, shush;
Shush, shush, shush; shush, shush, shush."
The mommies on the bus say, "Shush, shush, shush,"
All through the town.

If You're Happy and You Know It

If you're happy and you know it, clap your hands (clap clap),
If you're happy and you know it, clap your hands (clap clap),
If you're happy and you know it, then your face will surely show it,
If you're happy and you know it, clap your hands (clap clap).

If you're happy and you know it, stomp your feet (stomp stomp),
If you're happy and you know it, stomp your feet (stomp stomp),
If you're happy and you know it, then your face will surely show it,
If you're happy and you know it, stomp your feet (stomp stomp).

If you're happy and you know it, shout "Hurray!" (hoo-ray!),
If you're happy and you know it, shout "Hurray!" (hoo-ray!),
If you're happy and you know it, then your face will surely show it,
If you're happy and you know it, shout "Hurray!" (hoo-ray!)

If you're happy and you know it, do all three (clap-clap, stomp-stomp, hoo-ray!),
If you're happy and you know it, do all three (clap-clap, stomp-stomp, hoo-ray!),
If you're happy and you know it, then your face will surely show it,
If you're happy and you know it, do all three (clap-clap, stomp-stomp, hoo-ray!).

Before You Read

This song is thought to be an American folk song with no known writer. Do you ever wonder if there is a connection between the dog and the game of the same name?

Bingo

There was a farmer had a dog,
And Bingo was his name-o.
B-I-N-G-O!
B-I-N-G-O!
B-I-N-G-O!
And Bingo was his name-o!

There was a farmer had a dog,
And Bingo was his name-o.
(Clap)-I-N-G-O!
(Clap)-I-N-G-O!
(Clap)-I-N-G-O!
And Bingo was his name-o!

There was a farmer had a dog,
And Bingo was his name-o.
(Clap, clap)-N-G-O!
(Clap, clap)-N-G-O!
(Clap, clap)-N-G-O!
And Bingo was his name-o!

There was a farmer had a dog,
And Bingo was his name-o.
(Clap, clap, clap)-G-O!
(Clap, clap, clap)-G-O!
(Clap, clap, clap)-G-O!
And Bingo was his name-o!

There was a farmer had a dog,
And Bingo was his name-o.
(Clap, clap, clap, clap)-O!
(Clap, clap, clap, clap)-O!
(Clap, clap, clap, clap)-O!
And Bingo was his name-o!

There was a farmer had a dog,
And Bingo was his name-o.
(Clap, clap, clap, clap, clap)
(Clap, clap, clap, clap, clap)
(Clap, clap, clap, clap, clap)
And Bingo was his name-o!

90

Before You Read

The words and music to this song are anonymous. Usually kids sing this while touching all these body parts as they are named, and the song goes faster and faster until the kids collapse, laughing.

Head, Shoulders, Knees, and Toes

Head, shoulders, knees, and toes,

Knees and toes,

Head, shoulders, knees, and toes,

Knees and toes,

And eyes and ears and mouth and nose,

Head, shoulders, knees, and toes,

Knees and toes!

Before You Read

This is a Southern lullaby by an unknown author. It has been a popular lullaby to sing to a baby, repeatedly, until sleep arrives.

Hush, Little Baby

Hush, little baby, don't say a word,

Papa's gonna buy you a mockingbird.

And if that mockingbird don't sing,

Papa's gonna buy you a diamond ring.

And if that diamond ring turns brass,

Papa's gonna buy you a looking glass.

And if that looking glass gets broke,

Papa's gonna buy you a billy goat.

And if that billy goat won't pull,

Papa's gonna buy you a cart and bull.

And if that cart and bull turn over,

Papa's gonna buy you a dog named Rover.

And if that dog named Rover won't bark,

Papa's gonna buy you a horse and cart.

And if that horse and cart fall down,

You'll still be the sweetest little baby in town.

Old MacDonald Had a Farm

Old MacDonald had a farm, E-I-E-I-O!
And on his farm he had a cow, E-I-E-I-O!
With a "moo-moo" here and a "moo-moo" there
Here a "moo" there a "moo"
Everywhere a "moo-moo"
Old MacDonald had a farm, E-I-E-I-O

Old MacDonald had a farm, E-I-E-I-O
And on his farm he had a pig, E-I-E-I-O
With an "oink-oink" here and an "oink-oink" there
Here an "oink" there an "oink"
Everywhere an "oink-oink"
With a "moo-moo" here and a "moo-moo" there
Here a "moo" there a "moo"
Everywhere a "moo-moo"
Old MacDonald had a farm, E-I-E-I-O

Old MacDonald had a farm, E-I-E-I-O
And on his farm he had a horse, E-I-E-I-O
With a "neigh, neigh" here and a "neigh, neigh" there
Here a "neigh" there a "neigh"
Everywhere a "neigh-neigh"
With an "oink-oink" here and an "oink-oink" there
Here an "oink" there an "oink"
Everywhere an "oink-oink"
With a "moo-moo" here and a "moo-moo" there
Here a "moo" there a "moo"
Everywhere a "moo-moo"
Old MacDonald had a farm, E-I-E-I-O

Make New Friends, But Keep the Old

Make new friends, but keep the old;

One is silver, the other gold.

Circle is round, it has no end

That's how long I want to be your friend.

Make new friends, like new-made wine

Age will mellow and then refine.

I have a hand and you have another

Put them together and we've got each
other.

Over the mountains, under the sea

Friends forever we will always be.

Before You Read

This original song, a Christmas song, was written by American Lydia Maria Child in 1844. Another version is often sung at Thanksgiving time.

Over the River and Through the Woods

Over the river and through the woods,
To Grandmother's house we go.
The horse knows the way to carry the sleigh,
Through the white and drifted snow.

Over the river and through the woods,
Oh, how the wind does blow.
It stings the toes and bites the nose,
As over the ground we go.

Over the river and through the woods
To have a full day of play.
Oh, hear the bells ringing ting-a-ling-ling,
For it is Christmas Day.

Over the river and through the woods,
Trot fast my dapple gray;
Spring o'er the ground just like a hound,
For this is Christmas Day.

Over the river and through the woods,
And straight through the barnyard gate.
It seems that we go so dreadfully slow;
It is so hard to wait.

Over the river and through the woods,
Now Grandma's cap I spy.
Hurrah for the fun, the pudding's done;
Hurrah for the pumpkin pie.

Glossary

blithe: cheerful and carefree

bonny: good, attractive, robust

calico: brightly printed cotton fabric

crown: the top part of the head

curds and whey: Curds are like the lumps in cottage cheese, and whey is the part that does not form into curds.

duckling: a baby duck

dumpling: A small dough ball, sometimes baked around fruit; or it is someone cute, plump, and short.

faery/ fairy ring: A ring of mushrooms in the grass or a ring of darker grass (originally thought to be a place where fairies danced).

frock: a dress

frolicked: to run about playfully

haunches: In the case of a cat, a haunch is a back leg.

maw: mouth or jaws

mutton: sheep

nimble: quick and light in movement

ogre: In fairy tales, a giant who is evil and sometimes eats people!

porridge: like oatmeal

saveloy: a smoked sausage that is spicy

scarcely: almost not!

sixpence: an old British coin

sow: to plant seeds

spade: a digging tool, like a small shovel

stile: a step over a fence or wall

troll: from Scandinavian tales, a dwarf or giant that lives in caves or under bridges

trundle bed: a low bed that is kept under another bed

tuffet: a small mound in the grass, or a stool or low seat

waddle: to walk with short steps, tipping from side to side

wombat: a small, Australian animal that burrows in the ground

wren: a small songbird